PHRASES
for
PUBLIC SPEAKERS
and
PARAGRAPHS
for
STUDY

Compiled by

GRENVILLE KLEISER

First published in 1910

British Library Cataloguing-in-Publication Data
A catalogue record for this book is available
from the British Library

CONTENTS

AIMS AND PURPOSES OF SPEAKING

It is obvious that the style of your public speaking will depend upon the specific purpose you have in view. If you have important truths which you wish to make known, or a great and definite cause to serve, you are likely to speak about it with earnestness and probably with eloquence.

If, however, your purpose in speaking is a selfish one—if your object is self-exploitation, or to serve some special interest of your own—if you regard your speaking as an irksome task, or are unduly anxious as to what your hearers will think of you and your effort—then you are almost sure to fail.

On the other hand, if you have the interests of your hearers sincerely at heart—if you really wish to render a worthy public service—if you lose all thought of self in your heartfelt desire to serve others—then you will have the most essential requirements of true and enduring oratory.

-GRENVILLE KLEISER
Model Speeches for Practise, 1920

TO THE STUDENT

The experienced public speaker acquires through long practise hundreds of phrases which he uses over and over again. These are essential to readiness of speech, since they serve to hold his thought well together and enable him to speak fluently even upon short notice.

This book is one of practise, not theory. The student should read aloud daily several pages of these phrases, think just what each one means, and whenever possible till out the phrase in his own words. A month's earnest practise of this kind will yield astonishing results.

He should also study the paragraphs, reprinted here from notable speeches, and closely observe the use made of climax and other effects. The phrase and the paragraph are the principal elements in the public speaker's English style, and the student will be amply repaid for any time he devotes to their analysis.

GRENVILLE KLEISER

USEFUL PHRASES

A further objection to
Again, can we doubt
Again, we have abundant instances
Alas! how often
All experience evinces that
All that I have been stating hitherto
All that is quite true.
All this, I know well enough
All this is unnatural because
All we do know is that
Am I mistaken in this?
Amid so much that is uncertain
And, again, it is to be presumed that
And, finally, have not these
And, further, all that I have said
And hence it continually happens
And hence it is that
And here, in passing, let us notice
And here observe that
And if I know anything of
And if it is further asked why
And I sometimes imagine that
And I wish also to say that
And, in fact, it is
And it is certainly true
And it may be admitted that
And just here we touch the vital point in
And let me here again refer to
And now it begins to be apparent

And now we are naturally brought on to
And now we are told
And pursuing the subject
And so again in this day
And so, in like manner
And strange to say
And such, I say, is
And the same is true of
And the whole point of these observations is
And this is manifestly true
Any thoughtful man can readily perceive
As far as my experience goes
As for me, I say
As it were
At first it does seem as tho
At this very moment, there are
At times we hear it said.
Be it so.
Be true to your own sense of right.
Believe me, it is quite impossible for
But all is not done.
But bear in mind that
But by no kind of calculation can we
But do not tell me that
But further still
But here we take our stand.
But I am not quite sure that
But I digress.
But I do not desire to obtrude a
But I recollect that
But I shall go still farther.
But I submit whether it
But I will not dwell on
But I will not pause to point out
But if you look seriously at facts

But in any case
But in fact there is no reason for
But is it in truth so easy to
But is it rationally conceivable that
But it is fitting I should say
But, it may be urged, if
But lest it should still be argued that
But let it be once understood that
But let us suppose all these
But look at the difference.
But my idea of it is
But now, I repeat,
But now, lastly, let us suppose
But now let us turn to
But now, on the other hand, could
But now some other things are to be noted
But somehow all is changed!
But the question for us is
But to go still further
But waiving this assumption
But we dwell too long
But we have faith that
But what is the motive?
But what then?
But with us how changed!
But why do we speak of
But you may say truly
But you must remember
Can there be a better illustration than
Can you doubt it?
Certainly, I did not know
Compare now the case of
Did time admit I could show you
Does anybody believe that
Do you dream that

Do not entertain so weak an imagination
Do not misunderstand me.
Enough has been said of
Even apart from the vital question of
Everybody has to say that
Few people will dispute
First, sir, permit me to observe
For instance,
For instance, there surely is
For my part, I can say that I desire
For the sake of clearness
For this simple reason
For what?
Fortunately I am not obliged
From time to time
Happily for us
Has the gentleman done?
Have we any right to such a
He can not do it.
Heaven forbid!
Hence, I repeat, it is
Hence it is that
Hence, too, it has often, been said
Here I have to speak of
Here I wish I could stop.
Here it will be objected to me
Here let me meet one other question
History is replete with
How are we to explain this
How do you account for
I acknowledge the force of
I admire the indignation which
I admit it.
I admit, that if
I allude to

I am advised that already
I am aware that
I am distinctly maintaining
I am expecting to hear next
I am going to suggest
I am in sympathy with
I am justified in regarding
I am led to make one remark
I am mainly concerned with
I am myself of opinion that
I am naturally led on to speak of
I am no friend to
I am not arguing the
I am not ashamed to acknowledge
I am not complaining of
I am not denying that
I am not disposed to deny
I am not going to attempt to
I am not here to defend the
I am not insensible of
I am not justifying the
I am not speaking of exceptions.
I am not trying to absolve
I am obliged to mention
I am perfectly astounded at
I am perfectly confident that
I am perfectly indifferent concerning
I am persuaded that
I am quite certain that
I am sanguine that those who
I am speaking to-night for myself.
I am sure, at least, that
I am sure you will allow me
I am sure you will do me the justice
I am told that the reason

I am well aware that
I am willing to admit that
I appeal to you on behalf of
I ask how you are going to
I ask myself
I ask, then, as concerns the
I ask your attention to this point.
I assume that the argument for
I assume, then, that
I beg not to be interrupted here
I beg respectfully to differ from
I beg to assure you
I believe I speak the sentiment of
I believe in it as firmly as
I believe in the
I believe you feel, as I feel, that
I can not believe it.
I can not but feel that
I can not do better than
I can not even imagine why
I can not, therefore, agree with
I can not very well
I can scarcely conceive anything
I carry with me no hostile remembrance.
I certainly do not recommend
I come now to observe
I come, then, to this
I conclude that it was
I confess I can not help agreeing with
I confess my notions are
I confess that I like to dwell on
I confess truly
I dare say
I dare say to you
I differ very much from

I do not absolutely assert
I do not believe that
I do not blush to acknowledge
I do not contend that
I do not forget that
I do not know on what pretense
I do not mean to propose
I do not mean to say
I do not mistrust the future.
I do not overlook tho fact that
I do not pretend to believe
I do not question this.
I do not stand here before you
I do not think it unfair reasoning to
I do not vouch for
I do not want to argue the question of
I do not wish to be partial.
I do not wish you to suppose that
I do not yield to any one
I entirely agree upon this point.
I fear I only need refer to
I firmly believe that
I grant, of course, that
I grant that there are
I grant, too, of course, that
I have all along been showing
I have already alluded to
I have already said, and I repeat it
I have always argued that
I have another objection to
I have appealed to the testimony
I have a right to think that
I have been interested in hearing
I have been requested to say a word,
I have heard it said recently

15

I have hitherto been adducing instances
I have indicted
I have listened with pleasure to
I have never been able to understand
I have never fancied that
I have no confidence, then, in
I have no desire in this instance
I have no doubt that it is
I have only to add that
I have read of the
I have said that
I have so high a respect for
I have spoken of
I have the confident hope that
I have the strongest reason for
I have to appeal to you
I heartily hope and trust
I hope I have now made it clear that
I hope you will acquit me of
I insist that you do not
I invite you to consider
I know it is not uncommon for
I know that there is a difference of
I know that this will sound strange
I know well the sentiments of
I know whereof I speak.
I leave it to you to say.
I marvel that
I may as well reply
I may be told that
I may say further that
I may take it for granted
I mention them merely
I merely indicate
I must beg leave to dwell a moment

I must fairly tell you that
I must now beg to ask
I myself feel confident
I often wonder
I only wish to recognize
I pass by that.
I pass, then, from the question of
I personally doubt whether it
I plainly and positively state
I point you to
I proceed to inquire into
I quote from
I read but recently a story
I really can not think it necessary to
I recollect that
I rejoice at the change that
I remember once when
I reply with confidence that
I rest my opinion on
I said just now
I see no objection to
I see no reason to doubt
I shall ask you one question
I shall attempt to show
I shall content myself with asking
I shall not suffer myself to
I shall not undertake
I shall presently show
I shall sum up what has been said.
I shall, then, merely sum up
I share the conviction of
I should hold myself obliged to
I should not like to hold the opinion
I speak in the most perfect honesty
I speak only for myself.

I suppose most men will recollect
I take leave to say
I take the liberty of
I think I am right in saying
I think I can demonstrate that
I think it impossible that
I think it our duty
I think it well not to be disputed that
I think, on the contrary, that
I think that this is a great mistake.
I think these facts show that
I think we should be willing to
I trust it will not he considered ungenerous
I trust we are not the men to
I turn now to another reason why
I undertake to say
I use the word advisedly.
I venture to assert that
I venture to say
I venture to think
I want to invite your attention to
I want to know whether
I was astonished to learn
I was forcibly struck with one remark
I was very much struck with
I will allow more than this readily.
I will answer, not by retort, but by
I will call to mind this
I will go no further
I will not attempt to note the
I will not enter into details
I will not go into the evidence of
I will not stop to inquire whether
I will show you presently
I will speak but a word or two more.

I will suppose the objection urged
I wish I could state
I wish to call your attention to
I wish to know
I wish to say something about
I wish to observe that
I would not he understood as saying
I would not, indeed, say a word to extenuate
If any man were to tell me
If any one is so short-sighted
If I had my share
If I hesitate, it is because
If I insist on this point here
If I mistake not the sentiment of
If I must give an instance of this
If I read the signs of the time aright
If I were asked what it is that
If other evidence be wanting
If, perchance, one should say
If such a thing were possible
If such feelings were ever entertained
If such is the fact, then
If there is a man here
If we accept at all the argument
If we are conscious of
If we find that
If we resign ourselves to facts
If you want to find out what
If you wish the most conclusive proof
In a broader and a larger sense
In a sense, and a very real sense
In answer to this singular theory
In like manner
In order to carry out
In proof of this drift toward

In proportion as
In proportion, then,
In pursuance of these clear and express
In saying all this, I do not forget
In something of a parallel
In such cases
In support of this claim
In support of what I have been saying
In the first place
In the first place, then, I say
In the first place there is
In the last resort
In the light of these things
In this connection
In this point of view, doubtless
In this situation, let us
In this respect they are
In view of these facts, I say
In what I have to say
Is it fair to say that
Is it not evident that
Is it not quite possible that
Is it said that
Is not that the common sentiment?
Is there any reason for
It affords me unusual pleasure
It is but too true that
It can scarcely be imagined that
It can not be too often repeated
It certainly follows, then,
It does not appear to me
It has been maintained that
It has been more than hinted that
It has been said, and said truly,
It has sometimes been remarked that

It is a common observation that
It is a curious fact that
It is a fact patent to any one that
It is a melancholy fact that
It is a notorious fact that
It is a thing commonly said that
It is a very serious matter.
It is a very serious question
It is also to be borne in mind
It is amazing that there are any among us
It is an additional satisfaction
It is an undeniable truth that
It is apparent that
It is certain that
It is certainly not sufficient to say
It is difficult to conceive that
It is exceedingly unlikely that
It is historically certain that
It is in effect the reply of
It is in quite another kind, however,
It is, indeed, commonly said
It is more difficult to
It is necessary to account for
It is no more than fitting that
It is not a good thing to see
It is not a wise thing to
It is not alleged
It is not chiefly, however,
It is not for me here to recall
It is not, however,
It is not long since I had occasion
It is not my purpose to discuss
It is not necessary that I define
It is not proposed to
It is not surprizing that

It is not to be denied that
It is not told traditionally
It is not true that
It is not wonderful that
It is observable enough
It is of little consequence
It is of importance that
It is of very little importance what
It is quite true that
It is related of
It is singular that
It is the most extraordinary thing that
It is to my mind a
It is true, indeed, that
It is well known that
It is well that we clearly apprehend
It is wholly unnecessary
It is worthy of remark
It looks to me to be
It may be a matter of doubt
It may be shown that
It may be suggested that
It may be supposed that
It may in a measure be true that
It may not be improper for me to suggest
It must be borne in mind that
It must be confest that
It must be recollected that
It need hardly be said that
It remains for us to consider
It remains to
It remains to be shown that
It reminds me of an anecdote
It seems a truism to say
It seems now to be generally admitted

It should also be remembered that
It should be remembered
It so happens that
It was my good fortune
It was not so
It was under these circumstances
It were foolish to talk of
It were rash to say
It will be easy to cite
It will be found, in the second place,
It will be observed also that
It will be well to recall
It will not surely be objected
It would be misleading to say
It would be no less impracticable to
It would be vain to seek
It would do no good to repeat
It would seem that
Largely, I have no doubt, it is due
Let it be repeated
Let it be for an instant supposed
Let me add that
Let me ask who there is among us
Let me explain myself by saying
Let me illustrate
Let me instance in one thing only
Let me put the subject before you
Let me say one word further.
Let me tell you
Let me tell you a very interesting story
Let no one suppose that
Let the truth be said outright
Let these instances suffice
Let us bear in mind that
Let us consider that

Let us go a step further.
Let us say frankly
Let us see whether
Let us stand together.
Let us look a little at
Let us take an example in
Let us take, first of all,
Make no mistake.
Men are often doubtful about
Moreover, I am sure,
Moreover, I believe that
Much has been said of late about
My antagonism is only aroused when
My answer is, that
My belief is that
My own opinion is
Nay, further than this,
Need I speak of
Neither is it true that
Nevertheless, we must admit
Next I give you the opinion of
Next I observe that
No man who listens to me underrates
No matter what
No, no.
No objection can be brought against the
No one realizes this more
No one will, with justice, say
No one will question
No one would take the pains to challenge the
No wonder, then, that
Nobody really doubts that
Nor am I, believe me, so arrogant as
Nor can we imagine that
Nor is this surprizing

Nor, lastly, does this
Not a few persons demand
Not many words are required to show
Not quite so.
Not so here.
Nothing is more certain than
Nothing less.
Now, after what I have said,
Now apply this to
Now do you observe what follows from
Now for one moment let us
Now I have done.
Now, I proceed to examine
Now I want to ask whether
Now it is evident
Now let us observe what
Now, mark it.
Now, on the other hand, let me
Now perhaps you will ask me
Now we come to the question
Observe, if you please, that
Occasionally it is whispered that
Of course, it will be said that
Of no less import is
Of the final issue I have no doubt.
On the contrary
On the one hand
On the other hand
On the other hand, you will see
On the whole, then, I observe
One word more and I have done.
Once more, how else could
One fact is clear
Only a few days ago
Our position is that

Our position is unquestionable.
Over and over again it has been shown that
Perhaps, sir, I am mistaken in
Perhaps the reason of this may be
Permit me to add another circumstance
Permit me to remind you
Please remember that if
Readily we admit that
Since you have suffered me to
So far is clear, but
So it came naturally about
So much for
Some men think, indeed, that
Some persons have exprest surprize that
Something of extravagance there may be in
Strange as it may seem
Strictly speaking, it is not
Such an avowal is not
Such is not my theory.
Such is steadfastly my opinion that
Such is the truth.
Such, then, is the answer whir I make to
Supposing, for instance,
Surely I do not misinterpret the spirit
Surely it is preposterous
Surely, then,
Surely, this is good and clear reasoning.
Take, again, the case of
Take the instance of
That is quite obvious.
That we might have done.
The audacity of the statement is
The charge is false.
The conclusion is irresistible.
The contempt that is cast

The fact is substantially true.
The fact, is that there is not
The fact need not be concealed that
The facts are before us all
The first point to be ascertained is
The language is perfectly plain.
The least desirable form of
The more I consider this question
The plea serves well with
The point I wish to bring out
The problem that presents itself is
The question at issue is primarily
The question is not
The question presented is
The question with me is
The substance of all this is
The time is not far distant when
The time is short.
The truth of this has not been
Then, finally,
Then, I repeat,
There are many people nowadays who
There are people who tell you that
There is a cynicism which
There is a word which I wish to say
There is another reason why
There is another sense in which.
There is much force in
There is no danger of our overrating the
There is no evidence that
There is no good reason why
There is no mistaking the fact
There is no other intelligible answer
There is no parallel to
There is no sufficient reason for

There is none other.
There is not a shadow of
There is one other point connected with
There is one other point to which
There is something suggestive in
There was a time when none denied it.
These absurd pretensions
They did what they could.
This being the case, you will see
This brings me to a point on which
This does not mean
This expectation was disappointed.
This I have already shown
This is a great mistake.
This is it's last resort.
This is the only remaining alternative.
This leads me to the question
This relieves me of the necessity of
This is clearly perceived by
This is especially true of
This is essentially a question of
This is very different from
Tho all this is obvious
Thus, you see
To avoid all possibility of being
To be sure
To-day I have additional satisfaction in
To my own mind,
To my own mind, certainly, it is
To pass from that I notice
To take a very different instance
To this end we must
To this, likewise, it may be added
To this there can be but one answer.
To show all this is easy and certain.

To show this in fact
To sum up, then
Truly, gentlemen
Unless I am wholly wrong
Unless I greatly mistake the temper
We all remember
We are all aware that
We are here to discuss
We are now able to determine
We are told that
We can not leave unchallenged the
We deny it.
We have an instance in
We have no right to say
We, in our turn, must
We know they will not
We laugh to scorn the idea
We look around us
We may have an overpowering sense of
We may rest assured that
We must not propose in
We often speak of
We ought, first of all, to note
We should pause to consider
We will hear much in these days
We will not examine the proof of
What are you asked to do?
What are you going to do?
What can be more intelligible than
What do you say to
What do we understand by
What has become of it?
What is more remarkable still
What is the answer to all this?
What is this but an acknowledgment of

What is your opinion?
What then remains?
What we do say is
When all has been said, there remains
When I look around me
When it can be shown that
When it is recognized that
When that is said, all is said
When we contemplate the
When we reflect on these sentiments
Where there is prejudice, it is no use to argue.
Who finds fault with these things?
Why should an argument be required to prove that
Why should it be necessary to confirm
Will you tell me how
With possibly a single exception
With regard to what has been stated
Yet it is plain
Yet, strange to say,
You and I may hold that
You can not assert that
You can not invent a series of argument
You can not say that
You do not pretend that
You have the authority of
You know as well as I do
You may object at once, and say
You may object that
You may point, if you will, to
You may search the history of
You tell me that
You will say that

PARAGRAPHS FROM
NOTABLE SPEECHES

Let me here pause once more to ask whether the book in its genuine state, as far as we have advanced in it, makes the same impression on your minds now as when it was first read to you in detached passages; and whether, if I were to tear off the first part of it, which I hold in my hand, and give it to you as an entire work, the first and last passages, which have been selected as libels on the Commons, would now appear to be so when blended with the interjacent parts? I do not ask your answer—I shall have it in your verdict.

> THOMAS LORD ERSKINE.
> "Speech in Behalf of Stockdale."

Indeed, many of the statements we now read of the necessity of the wise governing the weak and ignorant are almost literal reproductions of the arguments advanced by the slaveholders of the South in defence of slavery just preceding the outbreak of the Civil War. That divergence from our original ideal produced the pregnant sayings of Mr. Lincoln, "A house divided against itself can not stand," and its corollary, "This nation can not permanently endure half slave and half free." He saw dearly that American democracy must rest, if it continued to exist, upon the ethical ideal which presided over its birth—that of the absolute equality of all men in political rights.

> WAYNE MACVEAGH.
> "Ideals in American Politics."

The idea of liberty is license; it is not liberty but it is license. License to do what? License to violate law, to trample constitutions under foot, to take life, to take property, to use the bludgeon and the gun or anything else for the purpose of giving themselves power. What statesman ever heard of that us a definition of liberty? What man in a civilized age has ever heard of liberty being the unrestrained license of the people to do as they please without any restraint of law or of authority? No man—no, not one—until we found the Democratic party, would advocate this proposition and indorse and encourage this kind of license in a free country.

> JOHN ALEXANDER LOGAN.
> "Self-government in Louisiana."

My countrymen, we do not now differ in our judgment concerning the controversies of past generations, and fifty years hence our children will be divided in their opinions concerning our controversies. They will surely bless their fathers and their fathers' God that the Union was preserved, that slavery was overthrown, and that both races were made equal before the law. We may hasten or we may retard, but we can not prevent the final reconciliation. Is it not possible for us now to make a truce with time, by anticipating and accepting its inevitable verdicts? Enterprises of the highest importance to our moral and material well-being invite us, and offer ample scope for the employment of our best powers. Let all our people, leaving behind them the battle-fields of dead issues, move forward, and, in the strength of liberty and a restored Union, win the grander victories of peace.

> JAMES ABRAM GARFIELD.
> "Inaugural Address."

I wish you, by the aid of the training which I recommend, to be able to look beyond your own lives and have pleasure in surroundings different from those in which you move. I want you to be able—and mark this point—to sympathize with other times, to be able to understand the men and women of other countries, and to have the intense enjoyment—an enjoyment which I am sure you would all appreciate—of mental change of scene. I do not only want you to know dry facts; I am not only looking to a knowledge of facts, nor chiefly to that knowledge. I want the heart to be stirred as well as the intellect. I want you to feel more and live more than you can do if you only know what surrounds yourselves. I want the action of the imagination, the sympathetic study of history and travels, the broad teaching of the poets, and, indeed, of the best writers of other times and other countries, to neutralize and check the dwarfing influences of necessarily narrow careers and necessarily stunted lives. That is the point which you will see I mean when I ask you to cultivate the imagination. I want to introduce you to other, wider, and nobler fields of thought, and to open up vistas of other worlds, when refreshing and bracing breezes will stream upon your minds and souls.

GEORGE JOACHIM GOSCHEN.
"On the Cultivation of the Imagination."

But it is a noteworthy fact that eminent qualities in men may often be traced to similar qualities in their mothers. Knowledge, it is true, is not hereditary, but high mental qualities are so, and experience and observation seem to prove that the transmission is chiefly through the mother's side. But leaving this physiological view, let us look at the purely educational. Imagine an educated mother training and molding the powers of her children, giving to them in the years of infancy those gentle yet permanent tendencies which are of more account in the formation of character than any subsequent educational influences, selecting for them the best instructors, encouraging and aiding them in their difficulties, rejoicing with them in their successes, able to take an intelligent interest in their progress in literature and science.

JOHN WILLIAM DAWSON.
"On the Higher Education of Women."

It only remains to remind you that another consideration has been strongly prest upon you, and, no doubt, will be insisted on in reply. You will be told that the matters which I have been justifying as legal, and even meritorious, have therefore not been made the subject of complaint; and that whatever intrinsic merit parts of the book may be supposed or even admitted to possess, such merit can afford no justification to the selected passages, some of which, even with, the context, carry the meaning charged by the information, and which, are indecent animadversions on authority.

THOMAS LORD ERSKIN.
"Speech in Behalf of Blockdale."

But let it now for argument's sake be admitted, saving always the reputation of honorable men who are not here to defend themselves—let it, I say, for argument's sake, be admitted that the gentlemen alluded to acted under the influence of improper motives. What then? Is a law that has received the varied assent required by the Constitution and is clothed with all the needful formalities thereby invalidated? Can you impair its force by impeaching the motives of any member who voted for it?

GOUVERNEUR MORRIS.
"Speech on the Judiciary."

Let us pause, sir, before we give an answer to this question. The fate of us, the fate of millions now alive, the fate of millions yet unborn, depend upon the answer. Let it be the result of calmness and intrepidity; let it be dictated by the principles of loyalty and the principles of liberty. Let it be such as never, in the worst events, to give us reason to reproach ourselves, or others reason to reproach us, for having done too much or too little.

JAMES WILSON.
"Vindication of the Colonies."

It is impossible to deny the facts, which were so glaring at the time. It is a painful thing to me, sir, to be obliged to go back to these unfortunate periods of the history of this war and of the conduct of this country; but I am forced to the task by the use which has been made of the atrocities of the French as an argument against negotiation. I think I have said enough to prove that if the French have been guilty we have not been innocent. Nothing but determined incredulity can make us deaf and blind to our own acts, when we are so ready to yield an assent to all the reproaches which are thrown out on the enemy, and upon which reproaches we are gravely told to continue the war.

CHARLES JAMES FOX.
"On the Rejection of Bonaparte's Overtures."

Now I think the people ought not to be made to wait for the relief they have a right to demand. They ought not to be made to suffer while we argue one another out of the recorded and inveterate opinions of our whole lives. I say, therefore, for myself, that, anxious to afford them all the relief which they require, regretting that the state of opinion around me puts it out of my power to afford that relief in the form I might prefer. I accommodate myself to my position, and make haste to do all that I can by the shortest way that I can. Consider how much better it is to relieve them to some substantial extent by this means, at once, than not to relieve at all, than not to initiate a system or measure of relief at all, and then go home at the end of this session of Congress, weak and weary, and spend the autumn in trying to persuade them that it was the fault of some of our own friends that nothing was done. How poor a compensation for wrongs to the people will be the victories over our friends!

RUFUS CHOATE.
"The Necessity of Compromises in American Politics."

It is of the very essence of true patriotism, therefore, to be earnest and truthful, to scorn the flatterer's tongue, and strive to keep its native land in harmony with the laws of national thrift and power. It will tell a land of its faults as a friend will counsel a companion. It will speak as honestly as the physician advises a patient. And if occasion requires, an indignation will flame out of its love like that which burst from the lips of Moses when he returned from the mountain and found the people to whom he had revealed the austere Jehovah and for whom he would cheerfully have sacrificed his life worshiping a calf.

THOMAS STARR KING.
"On the Privilege and Duties of Patriotism."

Our President is dead. He has served us faithfully and well. He has kept the faith; he has finished his course. Henceforth there is laid up for him a crown of glory, which the Lord, the righteous Judge, shall give him in that day. And He who gave him to us, and who so abundantly blest his labors, and helped him to accomplish so much for his country and his race, will not permit the country which He saved to perish. I believe in the overruling providence of God, and that, in permitting the life of our Chief Magistrate to be extinguished, He only closed one volume of the history of His dealings with this nation, to open another whose pages shall be illustrated with fresh developments of His love and sweeter signs of His mercy. What Mr. Lincoln achieved he achieved for us; but he left as a choice a legacy in his Christian example, in his incorruptible integrity, and in his unaffected simplicity, if we will appropriate it, as in his public deeds. So we take this excellent life and its results, and, thanking God for them, cease all complaining and press forward under new leaders to now achievements, and the completion of the great work which he who has gone left as a sacred trust upon our hands.

JOSIAH GILBERT HOLLAND.
"Eulogy of Abraham Lincoln."

Patriotism says, and says it in the interest of peace and economy and final fraternity, "Fight and conquer even at the risk of holding them for a generation under the yoke." Fight, tho, on such a scale that there will be no need of holding them; that they will gladly submit again to the rule which makes the republic one and blesses all portions with protection and with bounty. Fight till they shall know that they kick against fate and the resistless laws of the world! Patriotism calls on the Cabinet and the head of the nation and the generals who give tone to the campaign to forget the customs and interests of peace till we shall gain it by the submission of the rebels and the shredding of their last banner into threads.

THOMAS STARR KING.
"On the Privilege and Duties of Patriotism."

For myself, I believe that whatever estrangements may have existed in the past, or may linger among us now, are born of ignorance and will be dispelled by knowledge. I believe that of our forty-five States there are no two who, if they could meet in the familiarity of the intercourse, in the fulness of personal knowledge, would not only cease to entertain any bitterness, or alienation, or distrust, but each would utter to the other the words of the Jewish daughter, in that most exquisite of idylls which has come down to us almost from the beginning of time:

"Entreat me not to leave thee, or to return from following after thee; for whither thou guest, I will go; and where thou lodgest, I will lodge; thy people shall be my people, and thy God my God.

"Where thou diest, will I die, and there will I be buried; the Lord do so to me, and more also, if aught but death part me and thee."

GEORGE FRISBIE HOAR.
"Address at the Banquet of the New England Society."

He knew full well and displayed in his many splendid speeches and addresses that one unerring purpose of freedom and of union ran through her whole history; that there was no accident in it all; that all the generations, from the Mayflower down, marched to one measure and followed one flag; that all the struggles, all the self-sacrifice, all the prayers and the tears, all the fear of God, all the soul-trials, all the yearnings for national life, of more than two centuries, had contributed to make the country that he served and loved. He, too, preached, in season and out of season, the gospel of Nationality.

JOSEPH HODGES CHOATE.
"Oration on Rufus Choate."

I leave these fellows and turn for a moment to their victims. And I would here, without any reference to my own case, earnestly implore that sympathy with political sufferers should not be merely telescopic in its character, "distance lending enchantment to the view"; and that when your statesmen sentimentalize upon, and your journalists denounce, far-away tyrannies—the horrors of Neapolitan dungeons—the abridgment of personal freedom in continental countries—the exercise of arbitrary power by irresponsible authority in other lands—they would turn their eyes homeward and examine the treatment and the sufferings of their own political prisoners. I would in all sincerity suggest that humane and well-meaning men who exert themselves for the remission of the death-penalty as a mercy would rather implore that the doom of solitary and silent captivity should be remitted to the more merciful doom of an immediate relief from suffering by immediate execution— the opportunity of an immediate appeal from man's cruelty to God's justice.

STEPHEN JOSEPH MEANY.
"Legality of Arrest."

Do you ask me our duty as scholars? Gentlemen, thought, which the scholar represents, is life and liberty. There is no intellectual or moral life without liberty. Therefore, as a man must breathe and see before he can study, the scholar must have liberty first of all; and as the American scholar is a man and has a voice in his own government, so his interest in political affairs must precede all others. He must build his house before he can live in it. He must be a perpetual inspiration of freedom in politics. He must recognize that the intelligent exercise of political rights, which is a privilege in a monarchy, is a duty in a republic If it clash with his case, his retirement, his taste, his study, let it clash, but let him do his duty. The course of events is incessant, and when the good deed is slighted, the bad deed is done.

GEORGE WILLIAM CURTIS.
"The Duty of the American Scholar."

Let us, then, go straight forward to our duty, taking heed of nothing but the right. In this wise shall we build a work in accord with the will of Him who is daily fashioning the world to a higher destiny; a work resting at no point upon wrong or injustice, but everywhere reposing upon truth and justice; a work which all mankind will be interested in preserving in every age, since it will insure the increasing glory and well-being of mankind through all ages.

IGNATIUS DONNELLY.
"Reconstruction."

We are not only to do some things, but we are to do all things, and we are to continue so to do, so that the least deviation from the moral law, according to the covenant of works, whether in thought, word, or deed, deserves eternal death at the hand of God. And if one evil thought, if one evil word, if one evil action deserves eternal damnation, how many hells, my friends, do every one of us deserve whose lives have been one continued rebellion against God! Before ever, therefore, you can speak peace to your hearts, you must be brought to see, brought to believe, what a dreadful thing it is to depart from the living God.

GEORGE WHITEFIELD.
From Sermon, "On the Method of Grace."

I say we must necessarily undo these violent, oppressive acts. They must he repealed. You will repeal them. I pledge myself for it that you will in the end repeal them. I stake my reputation on it. I will consent to be taken for an idiot if they are not finally repealed. Avoid, then, this humiliating, disgraceful necessity. With a dignity becoming your exalted situation make the first advances to concord, to peace, and happiness; for that is your true dignity, to act with prudence and justice. That you should first concede is obvious, from sound and rational policy. Concession comes with better grace and more salutary effect from superior power. It reconciles superiority of power with the feelings of men, and establishes solid confidence on the foundations of affection and gratitude.

LORD CHATHAM.
"On Removing Troops from Boston."

For aught I know the next flash of electric fire that simmers along the ocean cable may tell us that Paris, with every fiber quivering with the agony of impotent despair, writhes beneath the conquering heel of her loathed invader. Ere another moon shall wax and wane the brightest star in the galaxy of nations may fall from the zenith of her glory never to rise again. Ere the modest violets of early spring shall ope their beauteous eyes the genius of civilization may chant the wailing requiem of the proudest nationality the world has ever seen, as she shatters her withered and tear-moistened lilies o'er the bloody tomb of butchered France.

JAMES PROCTOR KNOTT.
From Speech on "Duluth."

Among her noblest children his native city will cherish him, and gratefully recall the unbending Puritan soul that dwelt in a form so gracious and urbane. The plain house in which he lived—severely plain, because the welfare of the suffering and the slave were preferred to books and pictures and every fair device of art; the house to which the north star led the trembling fugitive, and which the unfortunate and friendless knew; the radiant figure passing swiftly through the streets, plain as the house from which it came, regal with royalty beyond that of kings; the ceaseless charity untold; the strong sustaining heart of private friendship; the eloquence which, like the song of Orpheus, will fade from living memory into a doubtful tale; that great scene of his youth in Faneuil Hall; the surrender of ambition; the mighty agitation and the mighty triumph with which his name is forever blended; the consecration of a life hidden with God in sympathy with man—these, all these, will live among your immortal traditions, heroic even in your heroic story. But not yours alone! As years go by, and only the large outlines of lofty American characters and careers remain, the wide republic will confess the benediction of a life like this, and gladly own that if with perfect faith and hope assured America would still stand and "bid the distant generations hail," the inspiration of her national life must be the sublime moral courage, the all-embracing humanity, the spotless integrity, the absolutely unselfish, devotion of great powers to great public ends, which were the glory of Wendell Phillips.

GEORGE WILLIAM CURTIS.
"Eulogy of Wendell Phillips."

No, it is something else than circumstances which makes us do God's will, just as it is something else than miracle which makes us believe His word. Miracle and circumstances do their part. They assist the heart; they make the task of the will easier; they do not compel obedience. He who has made us free respects our freedom even when we use it against Himself—even when we resist His own must gracious and gentle pressure and choose to disbelieve or to disobey Him. If Moses and the prophets are to persuade us—if we are not to be beyond persuasion, tho one rose from the dead—there must be that inward seeking, yearning after God, that wholeness of heart, that tender and affectionate disposition toward Him who is the end as He is the source of our existence, of which the Bible is so full from first to last—which is the very essence of religion—which He, its object and its author, gives most assuredly to all who ask Him.

HENRY PARRY LIDDON.
"The Adequacy of Present Opportunities."

Instantly under such an influence you ascend above the smoke and stir of this small local strife; you tread upon the high places of the earth and of history; you think and feel as an American for America; her power, her eminence, her consideration, her honor, are yours; your competitors, like hers, are kings; your home, like hers, is the world; your path, like hers, is on the highway of empires; our charge, her charge, is of generations and ages; your record, her record, is of treaties, battles, voyages, beneath all the constellations; her image, one, immortal, golden, rises on your eye as our western star at evening rises on the traveler from his home; no lowering cloud, no angry river, no lingering spring, no broken crevasse, no inundated city or plantation, no tracts of sand, arid and burning, on that surface, but all blended and softened into one beam of kindred rays, the image, harbinger, and promise of love, hope, and a brighter day!

RUFUS CHOATE.
"Oration on American Nationality."

I believe in woman-suffrage for the sake of woman herself. I believe in it because I am the son of a woman and the husband of a woman and the father of a prospective woman. I remember that at one of the first woman-suffrage meetings I ever attended one of the first speakers was an odd fellow from the neighboring town, considered half a lunatic. That didn't make much impression in those days when we were all considered a little crazy, but he was a little crazier than the rest of us. He pushed forward on the platform, seeming impatient to speak, and throwing his old hat down by his side, he said, "I don't know much about this subject nor any other; but I know this, my mother was a woman." I thought it was the best condensed woman-suffrage argument I ever heard in my life.

THOMAS WENTWORTH HIGGINSON.
"For Self-respect and Self-protection."

When the people complain they must either be right or in error. If they be right, we are in duty bound to inquire into the conduct of the ministers and to punish those who appear to have been most guilty. If they be in error, we ought still to inquire into the conduct of our ministers in order to convince the people that they have been misled. We ought not, therefore, in any question relating to inquiry, to be governed by our own sentiments. We must be governed by the sentiments of our constituents if we are resolved to perform our duty both as true representatives of the people and as faithful subjects of our king.

LORD CHATHAM.
"Second Speech on Sir Robert Walpole."

For this great evil some immediate remedy must be provided; and I confess, my lords, I did hope that his Majesty's servants would not have suffered so many years of peace to relapse without paying some attention to an object which ought to engage and interest all. I flattered myself I should see some barriers thrown up in defense of the constitution; some impediment formed to stop the rapid progress of corruption. I doubt not we all agree that something must be done. I shall offer my thoughts, such as they are, to the consideration of the House; and I wish that every noble lord that hears me would be as ready as I am to contribute his opinion to this important service. I will not call my own sentiments crude and undigested. It would he unfit for me to offer anything to your lordships which I had not well considered; and this subject, I own, has not long occupied my thoughts. I will now give them to your lordships without reserve.

LORD CHATHAM.
"Speech On the State of the Nation."

We have the freedom and freshness of a youthful nationality. We can trace out new paths which must be followed by our successors; we have a right to plant wherever we please the trees under shade of which they will sit. The independence which we thus enjoy, and the freedom to originate which we can claim, are in themselves privileges, but privileges that carry with them great responsibilities.

JOHN WILLIAM DAWSON.
"On the Progress of Science in Canada."

From your great cities and teeming prairies, from your learned altars and countless cottages, from your palaces on sea and land, from your millions on the waters and your multiplied millions on the plains, let one united cheering voice meet the voice that now comes so earnest from the South, and let the two voices go up in harmonious, united, eternal, ever-swelling chorus, Flag of our Union! wave on; wave ever! Ay, for it waves over freemen, not subjects; over States, not provinces; over a union of equals, not of lords and vassals; over a land of law, of liberty, and peace, not of anarchy, oppression, and strife!

BENJAMIN HARVEY HILL.
"On the Perils of the Nation."

It is really astonishing to hear such an argument seriously urged in this House. But, say these gentlemen, if you found yourself upon a precipice, would you stand to inquire how you were led there before you considered how to get off? No, sir; but if a guide had led me there I should very probably be provoked to throw him over before I thought of anything else. At least I am sure I should not trust to the same guide for bringing me off; and this, sir, is the strongest argument that can be used for an inquiry.

LORD CHATHAM.
"Speech on Sir Robert Walpole."

But let us hope for better things. Let us trust in that gracious Being who has hitherto held our country as in the hollow of his hand. Let us trust to the virtue and the intelligence of the people, and to the efficacy of religious obligation. Let us trust to the influence of Washington's example. Let us hope that that fear of heaven which expels all other fear, and that regard to duty which transcends all other regard, may influence public men and private citizens, and lead our country still onward in her happy career. Full of these gratifying anticipations and hopes, let us look forward to the end of that century which is now commenced. A hundred years hence other disciples of Washington will celebrate his birth, with no less of sincere admiration than we now commemorate it. When they shall meet, as we now meet, to do themselves and him that honor, so surely as they shall see the blue summits to his native mountains rise in the horizon, so surely as they shall behold the river on whose banks he lived, and on whose banks he rests, still flowing on toward the sea, so surely may they see, as we now see, the flag of the Union floating on the top of the capitol; and then, as now, may the sun in his course visit no land more free, more happy, more lovely, than this our own country!

DANIEL WEBSTER.
"The Character of Washington."

I am now talking of the invisible realities of another world, of inward religion, of the work of God upon a poor sinner's heart. I am now talking of a matter of great importance, my dear hearers; you are all concerned in it, your souls are concerned in it, your eternal salvation is concerned in it. You may be all at peace, but perhaps the devil has lulled you asleep into a carnal lethargy and security, and will endeavor to keep you there till he get you to hell, and there you will be awakened; but it will be dreadful to be awakened and find yourselves so fearfully mistaken, when the great gulf is fixt, when you will be calling to all eternity for a drop of water to cool your tongue and shall not obtain it.

GEORGE WHITEFIELD.
"On the Method of Grace."

Why, sir, have I been so careful in bringing down with great particularity these distinctions? Because in my judgment there are certain logical consequences following from them as necessarily as various corollaries from a problem in Euclid. If we are at war, as I think, with a foreign country, to all intents and purposes, how can a man here stand up and say that he is on the side of that foreign country and not be an enemy to his country?

> BENJAMIN FRANKLIN BUTLER.
> "Character and Results of War."

My lords, this awful subject, so important to our honor, constitution, and our religion, demands the most solemn and effectual inquiry. And again I call upon your lordships, and the united powers of the State, to examine it thoroughly and decisively and to stamp upon it an indelible stigma of the public abhorrence. And again I implore those holy prelates of our religion to do away these iniquities from among us. Let them perform an illustration; let them purify this House and this country from this sin.

> LORD CHATHAM.
> "The Attempt to Subjugate America."

Now, there are three questions before the people of the country to-day, and they are all public, all unselfish, all patriotic, all elevated, and all ennobling as subjects of contemplation and of action. They are the public peace in this large and general sense that I have indicated. They are the public faith, without which there is no such thing as honorable national life; and the public service, which unless pure and strong and noble makes all the pagans of free government but doggerel in our ears.

> WILLIAM MAXWELL EVARTS.
> "The Day We Celebrate."

47

Indeed, gentlemen, Washington's farewell address is full of truths important at all times, and particularly deserving consideration at the present. With a sagacity which brought the future before him, and made it like the present, he saw and pointed out the dangers that even at this moment most imminently threaten us. I hardly know how a greater service of that kind could now be done to the community than by a renewed and wide diffusion of that admirable paper, and an earnest invitation to every man in the country to reperuse and consider it. Its political maxims are invaluable; its exhortations to love of country and to brotherly affection among citizens, touching; and the solemnity with which it urges the observance of moral duties, and impresses the power of religious obligation, gives to it the highest character of truly disinterested, sincere, parental advice.

DANIEL WEBSTER.
"The Character of Washington."

Let no man dare, when I am dead, to charge me with dishonor; let no man attaint my memory by believing that I could have engaged in any cause but that of my country's liberty and independence; or that I could have become the pliant minion of power in the oppression or the miseries of my countrymen. The proclamation of the provisional government speaks for our views; no inference can be tortured from it to countenance barbarily or debasement at home, or subjection, humiliation, or treachery from abroad. I would not have submitted to a foreign oppressor for the same reason that I would resist the foreign and domestic oppressor; in the dignity of freedom I would have fought upon the threshold of my country, and its enemy should enter only by passing over my lifeless corpse. Am I, who lived but for my country, and who have subjected myself to the dangers of the jealous and watchful oppressor and the bondage of the grave only to give my countrymen their rights and my country her independence—am I to be loaded with calumny and not suffered to resent or repel it? No, God forbid!

ROBERT EMMET.
"Speech when under Sentence of Death."

When the law is the will of the people, it will be uniform and coherent; but fluctuation, contradiction, and inconsistency of councils must be expected under those governments where every evolution in the ministry of a court produces one in the State— such being the folly and pride of all ministers, that they ever pursue measures directly opposite to those of their predecessors.

SAMUEL ADAMS.
"American Independence."

I refer to the past not in malice, for this is no day for malice, but simply to place more distinctly in front the gratifying and glorious change which has come both to our white fellow citizens and ourselves and to congratulate all upon the contrast between now and then, the new dispensation of freedom with its thousand blessings to both races, and the old dispensation of slavery with its ten thousand evils to both races—white and black. In view, then, of the past, the present, and the future, with the long and dark history of our bondage behind us, and with liberty, progress and enlightenment before us, I again congratulate you upon this auspicious day and hour.

FREDERICK DOUGLASS.
"Inauguration of the Freedmen's
Memorial Monument to Abraham Lincoln."

In all popular tumults the worst men bear the sway at first. Moderate and good men are often silent for fear of modesty, who in good time may declare themselves. Those who have any property to lose are sufficiently alarmed already at the progress of these public violences and violations to which every man's dwelling, person, and property are hourly exposed. Numbers of such valuable men and good subjects are ready and willing to declare themselves for the support of government in due time, if government does not fling away its own authority.

LORD MANSFIELD.
"The Right of England to Tax America."

In jurisprudence, which reluctantly admits any new adjunct, and counts in its train a thousand champions ready to rise in defense of its formularies and technical rules, the victory has been brilliant and decisive. The civil and the common law have yielded to the pressure of the times, and have adopted much which philosophy and experience have recommended, altho it stood upon no test of the pandects and claimed no support from the feudal polity. Commercial law, at least so far as England and America are concerned, is the creation of the eighteenth century. It started into life with the genius of Lord Mansfield, and, gathering in its course whatever was valuable in the earlier institutes of foreign countries, had reflected back upon them its own superior lights, so as to become the guide and oracle of the commercial world.

JOSEPH STORY.
"Characteristics of the Age."

When that history comes to be written you know whose will be the central and prominent figure. You know that Mr. Gladstone will stand out before posterity as the greatest man of his time— remarkable not only for his extraordinary eloquence, for his great ability, for his stedfastness of purpose, for his constructive skill, but more, perhaps, than all these, for his personal character, and for the high tone that he has introduced into our politics and public fife. I sometimes think that great men are like great mountains, and that we do not appreciate their magnitude while we are close to them. You have to go to a distance to see which peak it is that towers above its fellows; and it may be that we shall have to put between us and Mr. Gladstone a space of time before we shall see how much greater he has been than any of his competitors for fame and power.

JOSEPH CHAMBERLAIN.
"On Liberal Aims."

Let us never despair of our country. Actual evils can be mitigated; bad tendencies can be turned aside; the burdens of government can be diminished; productive industry will be renewed; and frugality will repair the waste of our resources. Then shall the golden days of the republic once more return, and the people become prosperous and happy,

SAMUEL JONES TILDEN.
"Address on Administrative Reform."

Had Abraham Lincoln died from any of the numerous ills to which flesh is heir; had he reached that good old age to which his rigorous constitution and his temperate habits gave promise; had he been permitted to see the end of his great work; had the solemn curtain of death come down but gradually, we should still have been smitten with a heavy grief and treasured his name lovingly. But dying as he did die, by the red hand of violence; killed, assassinated, taken off without warning, not because of personal hate, but because of his fidelity to Union and liberty, he is doubly dear to us and will be precious forever.

FREDERICK DOUGLASS.
"Inauguration of the Freedmen's Memorial
Monument to Abraham Lincoln."

Let this be an occasion of joy. Why should it not be so! Is not the heaven over your heads, which has so long been clothed in sackcloth, beginning to disclose its starry principalities and illumine your pathway? Do you not see the pitiless storm which, has so long been pouring its rage upon you breaking away, and a bow of promise as glorious as that which succeeded the ancient deluge spanning the sky—a token that to the end of time the billows of prejudice and oppression shall no more cover the earth to the destruction of your race; but seedtime and harvest shall never fail, and the laborer shall eat the fruit of his hands. Is not your cause developing like the spring? Yours has been a long and rigorous winter. The chill of contempt, the frost of adversity, the blast of persecution, the storm of oppression—all have been yours. There was no substance to be found—no prospect to delight the eye or inspire the drooping heart—no golden ray to dissipate the gloom. The waves of derision were stayed by no barrier, but made a clear breach over you. But now—thanks be to God! that dreary winter is rapidly hastening away. The sun of humanity is going steadily up from the horizon to its zenith, growing larger and brighter, and melting the frozen earth beneath, its powerful rays. The genial showers of repentance are softly falling upon the barren plain; the wilderness is budding like the rose; the voice of joy succeeds the cotes of we; and hope, like the lark, is soaring upward and warbling hymns at the gate of heaven.

WILLIAM LLOYD GARRISON.
"From Words of Encouragement to the Opprest."

Listen to the voice of justice and of reason; it cries to us that human judgments are never certain enough to warrant society in giving death to a man convicted by other men liable to error. Had you imagined the most perfect judicial system; had you found the most upright and enlightened judges, there will always remain some room for error or prejudice. Why interdict to yourselves the means of reparation? Why condemn yourself to powerlessness to help opprest innocence? What good can come of the sterile regrets, these illusory reparations you grant to a vain shade, to insensible ashes? They are the sad testimonials of the barbarous temerity of your penal laws. To rob the man of the possibility of expiating his crime by his repentance or by acts of virtue; to close to him without mercy every return toward a proper life, and his own esteem; to hasten his descent, as it were, into the grave still covered with the recent blotch, of his crime, is in my eyes the most horrible refinement of cruelty.

MAXIMILIEN MARIE ISIDORE ROBESPIERRE.
"Against Capital Punishment."

And love, young men, love and venerate the ideal. The ideal is the word of God. High above every country, high above humanity, is the country of the spirit, the city of the soul, in which all are brethren who believe in the inviolability of thought and in the dignity of our immortal soul; and the baptism of this fraternity is martyrdom. From that high sphere spring the principles which alone can redeem the peoples. Arise for the sake of these, and not from impatience of suffering or dread of evil. Anger, pride, ambition, and the desire of material prosperity, are common alike to the peoples and their oppressors, and even should you conquer with these to-day, you would fall again to-morrow; but principles belong to the peoples alone, and their oppressors can find no arms to oppose them. Adore enthusiasm, the dreams of the virgin soul, and the visions of early youth, for they are a perfume of paradise which the soul retains in issuing from the hands of its Creator. Respect, above all things, your conscience; have upon your lips the truth implanted by God in your hearts, and, while laboring in harmony, even with those who differ from you, in all that tends to the emancipation of our soil, yet ever bear your own banner erect and boldly promulgate your own faith.

GIUSEPPE MAZZINI.
"To the Young Men of Italy."

Even if we conquer the South, as conquer we must, unless chastened by visible misfortunes in the North, our triumph breeding unbounded conceit, we plunge the deeper in the vortex of voluptuous prosperity, our country forgotten by the people, its honors and dignities the sport and plunder of every knave and fool that can court or bribe the mob, the national debt repudiated, justice purchased in her temples as laws now are in the Legislature, the life and property of no man safe, the last relics of public virtue destroyed, anarchy will reign amid universal ruin.

DANIEL DOUGHERTY.
"Address on the Perils of the Republic."

To conclude "How are the mighty fallen!" Fallen before the desolating hand of death. Alas, the ruins of the tomb! The ruins of the tomb are an emblem of the ruins of the world; when not an individual, but a universe, already marred by sin and hastening to dissolution, shall agonize and die! Directing your thoughts from the one, fix them for a moment on the other. Anticipate the concluding scene, the final catastrophe of nature, when the sign of the Son of man shall he seen in heaven; when the Son of man Himself shall appear in the glory of his Father, and send forth judgment unto victory. The fiery desolation envelops towns, palaces, and fortresses; the heavens pass away! the earth melts! and all those magnificent productions of art which ages heaped on ages have reared up are in one awful day reduced to ashes.

ELIPHALET NOTT.
"On the Death of Alexander Hamilton."

"Westward the course of empire takes its way;
The four first acts already past,
A fifth shall close the drama with the day:
Time's noblest offspring is the last."

This extraordinary prophecy may be considered only as the result of long foresight and uncommon sagacity; of a foresight and sagacity stimulated, nevertheless, by excited feeling and high enthusiasm. So clear a vision of what America would become was not founded on square miles, or on existing numbers, or on any common laws of statistics. It was an intuitive glance into futurity; it was a grand conception, which they have hitherto so hopelessly mismanaged, you must expect to go on from had to worse; you must expect to lose the little prestige which you retain; you must expect to find in other portions of the world the results of the lower consideration that you occupy in the eyes of mankind; you must expect to be drawn, on, degree by degree, step by step, under the cover of plausible excuses, under the cover of highly philanthropic sentiments, to irreparable disasters, and to disgrace that it will be impossible to efface.

LORD SALISBURY.
"Speech on the Abandonment of General Gordon."

You will pardon me, gentlemen, if I say I think that we have need of a more rigorous scholastic rule; such an asceticism, I mean, as only the hardihood and devotion of the scholar himself can enforce. We live in the sun and on the surface—a thin, plausible, superficial existence, and talk of muse and prophet, of art and creation. But out of our shallow and frivolous way of life, how can greatness ever grow? Come now, let us go and be dumb. Let us sit with our hands on our mouths, a long, austere, Pythagorean lustrum. Let us live in corners and do chores, and suffer, and weep, and drudge, with eyes and hearts that love the Lord. Silence, seclusion, austerity, may pierce deep into the grandeur and secret of our being, and so living bring up out of secular darkness the sublimities of the moral constitution. How mean to go blazing, a gaudy butterfly, in fashionable or political saloons, the fool of society, the fool of notoriety, a topic for newspapers, a piece of the street, and forfeiting the real prerogative of the russet coat, the privacy, and the true and warm heart of the citizen!

EMERSON.
"Literary Ethics."

Sir, we are assembled to commemorate the establishment of great public principles of liberty, and to do honor to the distinguished dead. The occasion is too severe for eulogy to the living. But, sir, your interesting relation to this country, the peculiar circumstances which surround you and surround us, call on me to express the happiness which we derive from your presence and aid in this solemn commemoration.

WEBSTER.
"Laying the Cornerstone of Bunker Hill Monument."

All experience teaches that the requirements and impartial practise of the principles of civil and religious liberty can not speedily be acquired by the inhabitants, left to their own way, under a protectorate by this nation. The experience of this nation in governing and endeavoring to civilize the Indians teaches this. For about a century this nation exercised a protectorate over the tribes and allowed the natives of the country to manage their tribal and other relations in their own way. The advancement in civilization, was very slow and hardly perceptible. During the comparatively few years that Congress has by direct legislation controlled their relations to each other and to the reservations the advancement in civilization has been tenfold more rapid. This is in accord with all experience. The un-taught can not become acquainted with the difficult problems of government and of individual rights and their due enforcement without skilful guides.

JONATHAN ROSS.
"The Nation's Relation to Its Island Possessions."

My friend, will you hear me to-day? Hark! what is He saying to you? "Come unto me, all ye that labor and are heavy laden, and I will give you rest. Take my yoke upon you and learn of me; for I am meek and lowly in heart; and ye shall find rest unto your souls. For my yoke is easy, and my burden is light." Will you not think well of such a Savior? Will you not believe in Him? Will you not trust in Him with all your heart and mind? Will you not live for Him? If He laid down His life for us, is it not the least we can do to lay down ours for Him? If He bore the cross and died on it for me, ought I not be willing to take it up for Him? Oh have we not reason to think well of Him? Do you think it is right and noble to lift up your voice against such, a Savior? Do you think it just to cry "Crucify Him! crucify Him!" Oh, may God help all of us to glorify the Father, by thinking well of His only-begotten Son.

DWIGHT LYMAN MOODY.
"What Think Ye of Christ?"

Life has been often styled an ocean and our progress through it a voyage. The ocean is tempestuous and billowy, overspread by a cloudy sky, and fraught beneath with shelves and quick-sands. The voyage is eventful beyond comprehension, and at the same time full of uncertainty and replete with danger. Every adventurer needs to be well prepared for whatever may befall him, and well secured against the manifold hazards of losing his course, sinking in the abyss, or of being wrecked against the shore.

TIMOTHY DWIGHT.
"The Sovereignty of God."

I shall endeavor to clear away from the question all that mass of dissertation and learning displayed in arguments which have been fetched from speculative men who have written upon the subject of government, or from ancient records, as being little to the purpose. I shall insist that these records are no proofs of our present constitution. A noble lord has taken up his argument from the settlement of the constitution at the revolution; I shall take up my argument from the constitution as it is now.

MANSFIELD.
"The Right of England to Tax America."

The rays from this torch illuminate a century of unbroken friendship between France and the United States. Peace and its opportunities for material progress and the expansion of popular liberties send from here a fruitful and noble lesson to all the world. It will teach the people of all countries that in curbing the ambitions and dynastic purposes of princes and privileged classes, and in cultivating the brotherhood of man, lies the true road to their enfranchisement. The friendship of individuals, their unselfish devotion to each other, their willingness to die in each other's stead, are the most tender and touching of human records; they are the inspiration of youth and the solace of age; but nothing human is so beautiful and sublime as two great peoples of alien race and language.

CHAUNCEY MITCHELL DEPEW.
"Oration at the Unveiling of the Bartholdi Statue."

With consciences satisfied with the discharge of duty, no consequences can harm you. There is no evil that we can not either face or fly from, but the consciousness of duty disregarded. A sense of duty pursues us ever. It is omnipresent, like the Deity. If we take to ourselves the wings of the morning, and dwell in the uttermost parts of the sea, duty performed, or duty violated, is still with us, for our happiness or our misery. If we say the darkness shall cover us, in the darkness as in the light our obligations are yet with us. We can not escape their power, nor fly from their presence. They are with us in this life, will be with us at its close; and in that scene of inconceivable solemnity, which lies yet further onward, we shall still find ourselves surrounded by the consciousness of duty, to pain us wherever it has been violated, and to console us so far as God may have given us grace to perform it.

WEBSTER.
"The Trial of John Francis Knapp for the Murder of Captain Joseph White."

In the short space of time spanned by a single life, as if by "the touch of the enchanter's wand," the people have built a government before which the mightiest realms of the earth pale their splendors as do the stars of night before the refulgent glory of the coming day. Population has increased from three to thirty millions. Instead of thirteen, thirty-one stars now shine in the clear blue of this glorious flag. The multitudinous pursuits of enlightened life are cultivated to their highest pitch. The press is mighty and free. Peace and contentment smile alike around the poor man's hearth and the rich man's hall. Education scatters its priceless gift to every home in the land. Religion gathers around its altars the faithful of every creed. Statesmen have arisen "fit to govern all the world and rule it when 'tis wildest." Orators have appeared who have rivaled the great masters of antiquity. The doors of the American Parthenon are ever open to invite the humble but aspiring youth to enter and fill the loftiest niche. The highest dignity is within the grasp of all; for the lowly boy, born and reared in our own sweet valley of Cumberland, shall, when the spring comes round again, be clothed by the people with the first of mortal honors—that of guiding for a time the American republic upon her highway of glory.

DANIEL DOUGHERTY.
"Oration on Democracy."